Contents

What is wood?   6

How we get wood   8

What is wood like?   10

Wood for fuel   12

Wood in buildings   14

Wood indoors   16

Wooden furniture   18

Shaping wood   20

Paper   22

Wood in boats   24

Saving trees   26

Glossary   28

Index   30

Words in **bold** are in the glossary.

What is wood?

Wood is a **natural material**. It comes from the trunks and branches of trees.

We use wood to make lots of different objects.

This garden furniture is made from wood.

The outside of these pencils is made from wood.

How we **USE** materials

Wood

Holly Wallace

W
FRANKLIN WATTS
LONDON·SYDNEY

First published in 2006 by
Franklin Watts
338 Euston Road
London NW1 3BH

Franklin Watts Australia
Hachette Children's Books
Level 17/207 Kent Street
Sydney NSW 2000

Art director: Jonathan Hair
Series designed and created for Franklin Watts by Painted Fish Ltd.
Designer: Rita Storey
Editor: Fiona Corbridge
Picture credits
Corbis/Natalie Fobes p. 8 (left); Corbis/Paul A. Souders p. 24; Corbis/Amet Jean
Pierre p. 25 (bottom); Greenpeace p. 26, p. 27 (top); istockphoto.com p. 6 (right), p.
8 (right), p. 11 (top), p. 14, p. 15 (bottom), p. 17 (top), p. 18, p. 27 (bottom); Tudor
Photography p. 6 (left), p. 7 (bottom), p. 10, p. 11 (bottom), p. 12, p. 13, p. 15 (top),
p. 19 (top), p. 20, p. 21 (bottom), p. 22, p. 23; Wood for Good p. 9 (top), p. 16, p. 17
(bottom), p. 19 (bottom); www.ukmirrorsailing.com p. 25 (top).

Cover images: Tudor Photography, Banbury

ISBN-10: 0 7496 6457 6
ISBN-13: 978 0 7496 6457 2
Dewey classification: 674

A CIP catalogue record for this book is available from the British Library.

Printed in China

Wood is good for making things because it is hard and strong. It is easy to cut into different shapes, such as this picture frame and these spoons. Wood is also nice to look at.

Wood keywords

Natural
Hard
Strong

Look around you. How many things can you see that are made of wood?

How we get wood

We have to chop down trees and cut them up into pieces to use their wood.

We use big machines to chop down trees. The trees are taken to a **sawmill** to be cut up.

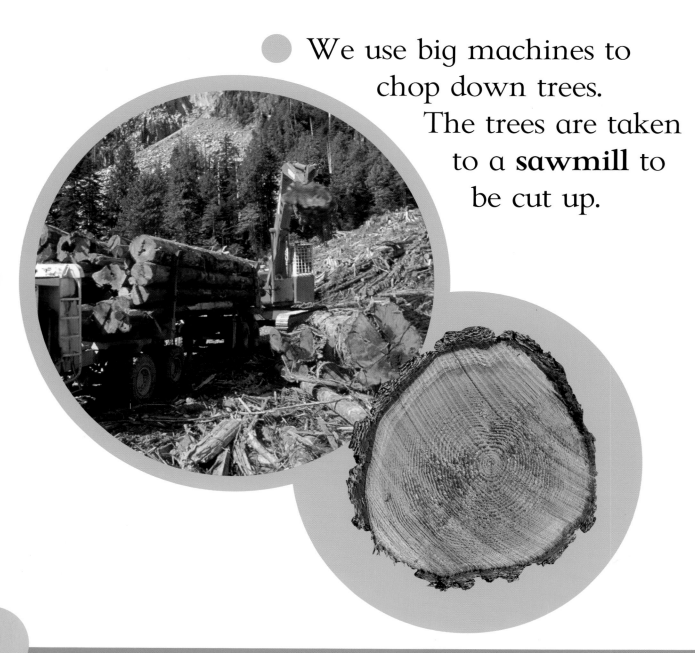

At the sawmill, workers use powerful **saws** to saw (cut) the trees into **planks**.

When trees are sawn up, lots of tiny pieces of wood are left, called sawdust. Sawdust makes a cosy bed for a pet.

Wood keywords
Saw
Sawmill
Sawdust
Planks

What is wood like?

There are many kinds of trees. We get different kinds of wood from them.

- Some wood is very hard and strong. It will last for a long time. It is used to make furniture such as tables.

- Some wood is softer. These boxes are made from wood that can be **bent** easily.

Wood has a pattern on it called the grain. Each kind of tree has a different grain. Some are very beautiful.

Wood keywords

Soft
Bent
Grain

We use wood to make things that are good to touch and look at, such as this chessboard.

Wood for fuel

We use wood as a fuel. This means that we burn it to give us heat or power.

We can make a fire by burning wood. People chop wood into **logs** to burn. Fires keep us warm. We can also use them to cook on.

Wood only burns when it is dry. If wood is damp, it is hard to set alight.

Wood keywords
Fuel
Burn
Charcoal
Logs

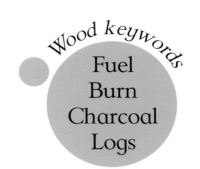

Charcoal is made from burned wood. It is a good fuel for cooking food because it burns slowly.

Wood in buildings

Wood is a strong material. This makes it very useful for building.

Builders use wood for **frames** that help to hold up parts of a building. This frame is the base for a roof.

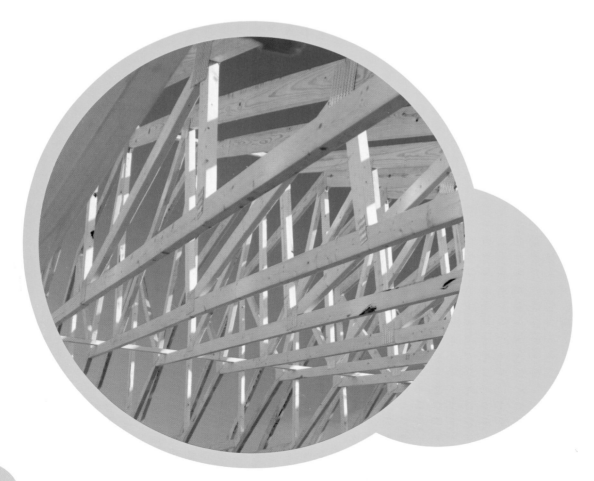

Wood rots if it gets wet. Wood used outside has to be protected. This shed has been painted with a **chemical** to stop it **rotting**.

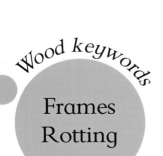

Wood keywords

Frames
Rotting

Paint is also used to help protect wood. This wooden fence has been painted.

Wood indoors

Builders use wood inside our houses, too. Floors, doors, stairs and window frames are made of wood.

How many other wooden objects can you find in your home?

● Look for shelves, cupboards and **skirting boards**. You might have a wooden kitchen worktop like this one.

Wood is cut into thick planks to make **floorboards**. These are strong so they can carry the heavy furniture we put on our floors.

Chips of wood can be mixed with glue to make boards called **chipboard** or MDF. Some kitchen cupboards are made of boards like this.

Wood keywords
Planks
Floorboards
Chipboard

Wooden furniture

Wood is easy to cut into different shapes and to join together, so it is good for making furniture.

We make tables and chairs from wood. The bed you sleep in may be made from wood, too.

This chair is made out of wood. It is **solid** and strong so it will not break when someone sits on it.

We can **polish** the **surface** of wooden furniture to make it shine, or use shiny **varnish** to protect it. We can also paint it with different colours. This table is polished.

Very thin sheets of wood are glued together to make **plywood**. This is light and strong. We can use it for desks and bookcases.

Wood keywords
Solid
Polish
Plywood
Varnish

Shaping wood

We can cut sheets of wood into different shapes and fix them together. This violin is made of different shapes.

We can take a solid block of wood and use tools to cut and shape it. This is called carving. These teddy bear bookends have been carved.

Some wood can be bent to make shapes like the back of this chair.

This wooden bowl was shaped by a machine. The machine made a piece of wood spin around quickly and a tool cut it into a bowl shape. This is called turning.

Wood keywords

Carving
Turning

21

Paper

Paper is made from tiny pieces of wood mixed with chemicals and water. This makes a soggy **pulp**. It is rolled out and dried to make paper. We use paper for many things.

Most paper is made into books, newspapers and magazines. It is also used to make card, cardboard, bags and wrapping paper.

Paper is good for making disposable things. These are things we use once and throw away, such as this cup and plate.

Factories use paper and card to hold and protect the things they make. This is called packaging.

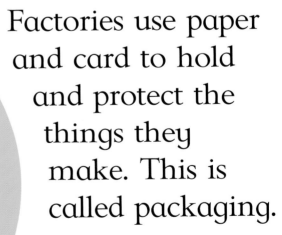

Wood keywords

Pulp
Cardboard
Paper
Card

Wood in boats

Wood is used to make boats. Wood **floats**, it is strong and it looks good.

A boat-builder cuts and shapes the pieces of wood for the boat. Then he joins them together tightly to stop water getting inside the boat.

Wooden boats must be painted or varnished to make them **waterproof**. Otherwise the wood will rot when it gets wet.

Wood keywords

Floats
Waterproof
Teak

The deck (floor) of this boat is made from an expensive kind of wood called teak. It has been varnished to protect it.

Saving trees

Trees take a long time to grow. If we cut down too many trees, some kinds of wood will run out.

In the **rainforests**, people are cutting down too many trees.

Rainforests are useful because they use up **carbon dioxide** and give out **oxygen**.

Many different plants and animals, such as this jaguar, live in rainforests. If we cut down the forests, the animals will disappear.

Wood keywords

Oxygen
Carbon dioxide
Rainforests

It is best to cut down trees that are specially grown for their wood.

Glossary

Bent Made into a curved shape.

Boards Flat pieces of wood and other materials.

Carbon dioxide One of the gases in the air. We breathe out carbon dioxide.

Chemical A substance that can be used to do many jobs, including stopping wood from rotting.

Chipboard Flat boards made from small pieces of wood called chips.

Floats Stays on the surface of water and does not sink.

Floorboards Long, thin planks of wood used to make floors.

Frames Pieces of wood joined together to make a structure. In a building, frames help to hold up parts of the building. A picture frame is four pieces of wood joined to make a border for a picture.

Logs Chopped-up branches and tree trunks.

Natural material Comes from the Earth, plants or animals.

Oxygen One of the gases in the air. We breathe in oxygen.

Planks Long, flat pieces of wood made when a tree is cut up.

Plywood Thin sheets of wood that are glued together.

Polish To rub the surface of wood so that it shines, using a waxy material called polish.

Pulp A soggy material made from wood mixed with water and chemicals. It is used to make paper.

Rainforests Thick forests that grow in parts of the world where it is always warm and wet.

Rotting Going soft and crumbly.

Saws Sharp tools used to cut wood.

Sawmill A factory where trees are cut into planks with saws.

Skirting boards Pieces of wood fixed along the bottom of a wall inside a house.

Solid Firm and fixed in shape.

Substance The matter or material that a thing is made up of.

Surface The top or outer layer of something.

Varnish A liquid that can be painted on wood to protect it. Varnish can be shiny or dull.

Waterproof Does not let water pass through.

Index

animals 27

bent wood 10, 21, 28
boards 17, 28
boats 24, 25
buildings 14, 15

carbon dioxide 27, 28
card 22, 23
cardboard 22
carving 20
charcoal 13
chemicals 15, 22, 28
chipboard 17, 28
chips 17, 28

fire 12
floorboards 17, 25, 28
frames 14, 16, 28
fuel 12, 13
furniture 6, 10, 18, 19

grain 11

houses 16

logs 12, 28

MDF 17

natural materials 6, 28

oxygen 27, 28

packaging 23
paint 15, 19, 25
paper 22, 23
picture frames 7, 28
planks 9, 17, 29
plants 27
plywood 19, 29
polish 19, 29
pulp 22, 29

rainforests 26, 27, 29

rot 15, 25, 29

sawdust 9
sawmills 8, 29
saws 9, 29
shapes 7, 20, 21
sheds 15
skirting boards 16, 29
surfaces 19, 29

teak 25
trees 6, 8, 10, 26, 27
turning 21

varnish 19, 25, 29

waterproof 25, 29
worktops 16